CANTIQUE DE NOËL
(O Holy Night)

T0048395

2

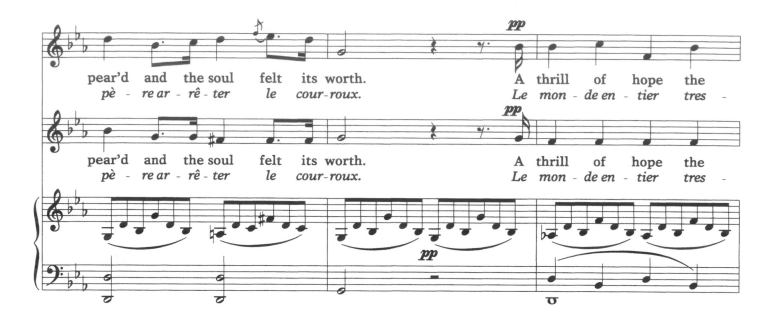

pear'd and the soul felt its worth.
pè - re ar - rê - ter le cour-roux.
A thrill of hope the
Le mon - de en - tier tres -

wea - ry world re-joi - ces, For yon - der breaks a new and glo - rious morn. __
sail - le d'e - spé-ran - ce A cet - te nuit qui lui don-ne un Sau-veur. __

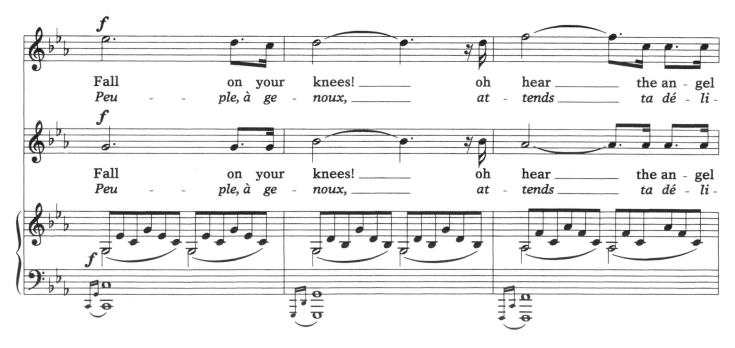

Fall on your knees! _____ oh hear _____ the an - gel
Peu - - ple, à ge - noux, _____ at - tends _____ ta dé - li-

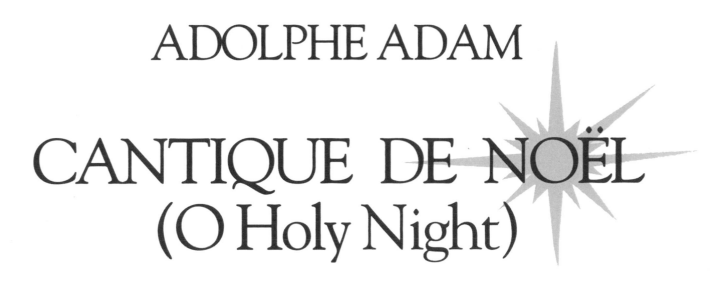

ADOLPHE ADAM

CANTIQUE DE NOËL
(O Holy Night)

Soprano, Alto, and Piano
Soprano, Tenor, and Piano
(arranged by Carl Deis)

G. SCHIRMER, _Inc._

DISTRIBUTED BY

HAL•LEONARD®
CORPORATION

7777 W. BLUEMOUND RD. P.O. BOX 13819 MILWAUKEE, WI 53213

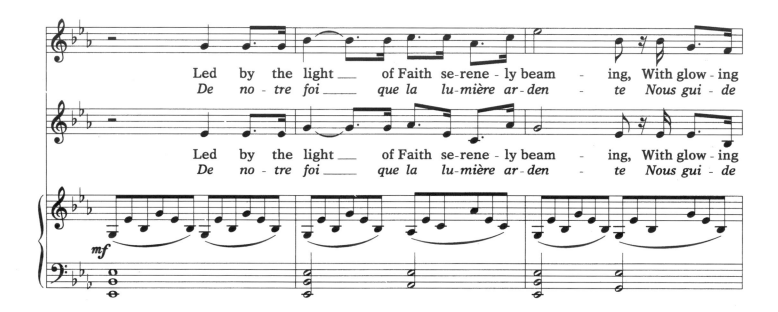

Led by the light ___ of Faith se-rene - ly beam - ing, With glow - ing
De no - tre foi ___ que la lu-mière ar - den - te Nous gui - de

Led by the light ___ of Faith se-rene - ly beam - ing, With glow - ing
De no - tre foi ___ que la lu-mière ar - den - te Nous gui - de

hearts by his cra - dle we stand. So led by
tous au ber-ceau de l'en-fant. Comme au - tre-

hearts by his cra - dle we stand. So led by
tous au ber-ceau de l'en-fant. Comme au - tre-

light of a star sweet-ly gleam - ing Here came the wise __ men from the O - rient
fois une é-toi - le bril-lan - te Y con-dui-sit les chefs __ de l'o - ri-

light of a star __ sweet-ly gleam - ing Here came the wise __ men from the O - rient
fois une é-toi - le bril-lan - te Y con-dui-sit les chefs __ de l'o - ri-

land. The King of kings lay thus in low - ly man - ger, In
ent. Le Roi des rois naît dans une hum - ble crè - che. Puis-

land. The King of kings lay thus in low - ly man - ger, In
ent. Le Roi des rois naît dans une hum - ble crè - che. Puis-

all our tri - als born to be our friend, __ He knows our
sans du jour, fiers de vo-tre gran-deur, __ À vo - tre or-

all our tri - als born to be our friend, __ He knows our
sans du jour, fiers de vo-tre gran-deur, __ À vo - tre or-

need, _____ he guard - - eth us from dan - ger; Be-
gueil   c'est de là   qu'un Dieu prê - che, Cour-

need, _____ he guard - - eth us from dan - ger; Be -
gueil   c'est de là   qu'un Dieu prê - che, Cour-

hold _____ your King! _____ be - fore _____ the low - ly
bez _____ vos fronts _____ de - vant _____ le Ré - demp-

hold _____ your King! _____ be - fore _____ the low - ly
bez _____ vos fronts _____ de - vant _____ le Ré - demp-

bend,   Be-hold   your King,   your
teur,   Cour-bez   vos fronts   de -

bend,   Be-hold   your King, _____ your
teur,   Cour-bez   vos fronts _____ de -

cresc.

7

King,   be - fore ___ him   bend.
vants   le ___ Ré-demp-teur.

King,   be - fore ___ him   bend.
vants   le ___ Ré-demp-teur.

Tru - ly   he   taught us   to love   one an-oth - er; His law   is
Le   Ré-demp-teur   a   bri-sé   toute en-tra - ve, La terre est

Tru - ly   he   taught us   to love_ one an-oth - er; His law   is
Le   Ré-demp-teur   a   bri-sé___ toute en-tra - ve, La terre est

love, and his Gos - pel is Peace.   Chains shall he
li - bre et le ciel est ou - vert.   *Il voit un*

break, for the slave is our bro - ther, And in his name all op - pres - sion shall
frè - re où n'é - tait qu'un es - cla - ve, L'a-mour u - nit ceux qu'en-châi - nait le

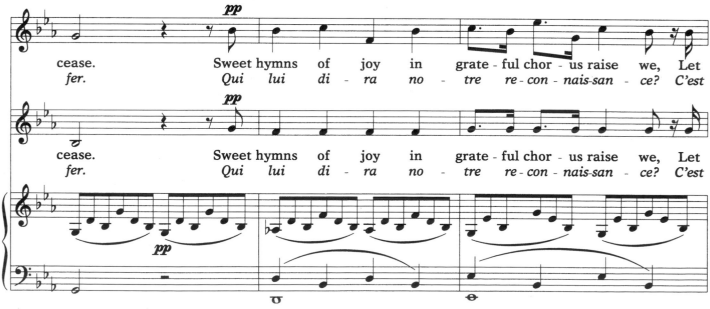

cease.   Sweet hymns of joy in grate - ful chor - us raise we, Let
fer.   *Qui lui di - ra no - tre re - con - nais-san - ce? C'est*

all with - in us praise his ho - ly name. ___ Christ is the
pour nous tous qu'il naît, qu'il souf - fre et meurt. ___ *Peu* - - *ple de-*

Lord, then ev - er, ev - er praise we, His
bout, *chan* - *te ta dé - li - vran* - *ce.* *No-*

pow'r ___ and glo - - ry ___ ev - - er-more pro-
ël! ___ *No - ël!* ___ *chan* - *tons* ___ *le Ré - demp-*

claim,   His pow'r _____ and glo   -   -   -   ry
teur,   No - ël! _____ No - ël! _____ chan-

claim,   His pow'r _____ and glo   -   -   -   ry
teur,   No - ël! _____ No - ël! _____ chan

cresc.

rall.   *a tempo*

ev - er - more _ pro-claim.
tons   le _ Ré-demp-teur.

rall.   *a tempo*

ev - er - more _ pro-claim.
tons   le _ Ré-demp-teur.

rall.   *a tempo*

ff *marc.*

CANTIQUE DE NOËL
(O Holy Night)

Adolphe Adam
arranged by Carl Deis

Copyright © 1935 (renewed), 1950 (renewed) by G. Schirmer, Inc. (ASCAP) New York, NY
All Rights Reserved. International Copyright Secured.
Warning: Unauthorized reproduction of this publication is
prohibited by Federal law and subject to criminal prosecution.

vine!_____ O night, O_____ night di-vine!
ël!_____ voi - ci le_____ Ré-demp-teur.

vine!_____ O night, O night di-vine!
ël!_____ voi - ci le Ré-demp-teur.

Led by the
De no - tre

With glow - ing hearts by His cra - dle we
Nous gui - de tous au ber-ceau de l'en-

light__ of Faith se-rene-ly beam - ing, With glow-ing hearts by His cra-dle we
foi__ que la lu-miè-re ar-den - te Nous gui-de tous au ber-ceau de l'en-

stand;
fant,

stand;
fant,

So, led by light of a star sweet-ly
Com-me au-tre-fois une é-toi-le bril-

Here came the wise men from the O-rient land.
Y con - dui - sit les chefs de l'o - ri - ent.

gleam - ing, Here came the wise men from ___ the O-rient land. The
lan - te Y con-dui-sit les chefs___ de l'o - ri - ent. Le

cresc.

In all our tri - als
Puis sants du jour,_____ fiers

King of Kings lay thus in low-ly man-ger, In all our tri - als
Roi des Rois naît dans une hum-ble crè - che; Puis-sants du jour, fiers

cresc.

cresc.

Love and His Gos - pel is Peace. Chains shall He
li - bre et le ciel est ou - vert. Il voit un

Love and His Gos - pel is Peace. Chains shall He
li - bre et le ciel est ou - vert. Il voit un

break, for the slave is our broth - er, And in His name all op - pres - sion shall
frè - re où n'é-tait qu'un es - cla - ve, L'amour u - nit ceux qu'en-chaî - nait le

break, for the slave is our broth - er, And in His name all op - pres - sion shall
frè - re où n'é-tait qu'un es - cla - ve, L'amour u - nit ceux qu'en-chaî - nait le

cease. Sweet hymns of joy in grate-ful cho-rus raise we, Let
fer. Qui lui di - ra no - tre re-con-nais-san - ce? C'est

cease. Sweet hymns of joy in grate-ful cho-rus raise we, Let
fer. Qui lui di - ra no - tre re-con-nais-san - ce? C'est

COMPLETE LISTING OF G. SCHIRMER EDITIONS OF "CANTIQUE DE NOEL"

VOCAL SOLO (French and English)

50279730	High in E flat with Piano (Adam/Deis)
50285970	Medium High in D flat with Piano (Adam/Deis)
50281510	Medium in C with Piano (Adam/Deis)
50279740	Low in B flat with Piano (Adam/Deis)
50290250	High in E flat with Organ (Adam/Stickles)
50290240	Medium High in D flat with Organ (Adam/Stickles)
50290230	Medium Low in C with Organ (Adam/Stickles)
50290220	Low in B flat with Organ (Adam/Stickles)

VOCAL DUET (French and English)

50483073	Soprano/Alto and Soprano/Tenor in one edition (Adam/Deis)

CHORAL

50304340	SATB/Piano with Soprano and Tenor Solo (Adam/Buck)
50293890	SATB/Organ with Soprano and Tenor Solo (Adam/Buck)
50304200	SAB/Piano (Adam/Deis)

SOLO KEYBOARD

50281610	Solo Organ (Adam/Nobel)
50285510	Simplified Piano (Adam/Steiner)

0-73999-65116-4

HL50483073

G. SCHIRMER, Inc.

DISTRIBUTED BY

HAL•LEONARD®
CORPORATION

7777 W. BLUEMOUND RD. P.O. BOX 13819 MILWAUKEE, WI 53213

U.S. $7.99

ISBN 978-0-7935-8275-4

50799

9 780793 582754